Spot the Difference SPORTS!

A Fun Picture Puzzle Books for Children Age 6-10

by Raphael Dali

Find 5 Differences in each puzzles
Can you find them all?

Copyright 2023 By Raphael Dali. All rights reserved.
No part of this book may be reproduced in any form or by any electronic or mechanical means, including information storage and retrieval systems, without written permission from the author, except for the use of brief quotations in a book review.

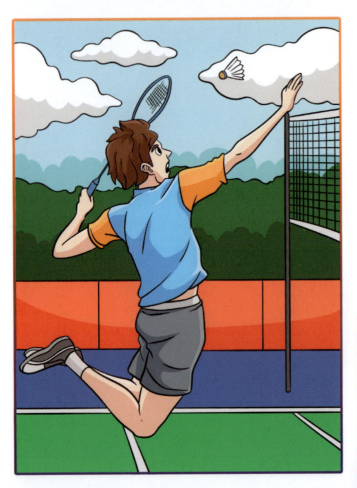

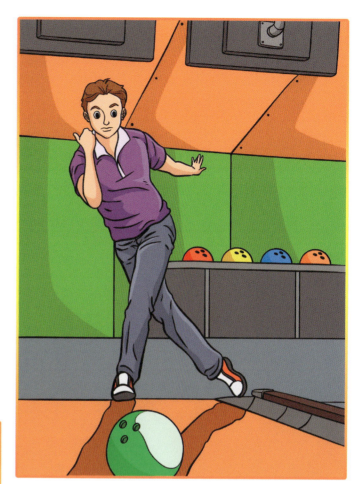

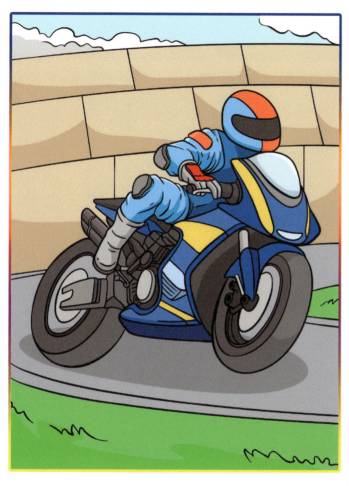

ANSWER

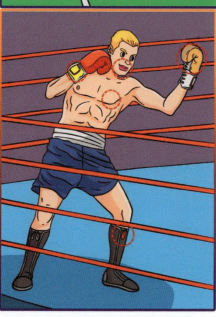
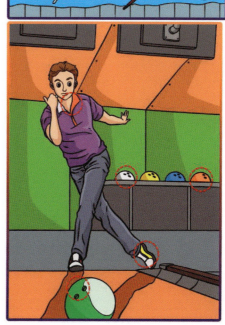

Printed in Great Britain
by Amazon